Avalanche Dog Heroes

Piper and Friends Learn to Search the Snow

Elizabeth Rusch

little bigfoot

an imprint of sasquatch books
seattle, wa

When you wake in the morning to a white, snow-blanketed world, you may be excited to get a day off school.

But every snow day is a school day for Piper, Sara Cohen's three-year-old border collie. Piper goes to school at Crystal Mountain Resort in Washington, where she and her canine friends are training for a heroic job: finding people buried under snow.

Steep slopes and heavy snowfall draw thousands of people to Crystal Mountain every winter to ski and snowboard. But steep terrain and snowstorms also cause avalanches—massive slides of snow and ice that can knock people over and completely cover them.

Two Main Types of Avalanches

LOOSE SNOW AVALANCHE

Loose snow avalanches start at one point, where something like a person's weight pushes the snow. As the loose snow slides downhill, the avalanche collects more snow and widens. These avalanches tend to be smaller and less dangerous, but people can still get trapped.

SLAB AVALANCHE

More dangerous avalanches occur when a large slab of snow cracks off in one piece and slides. It's a little like a book sliding off a tilted table. The slab might start moving at twenty miles per hour. But it can reach up to eighty miles per hour as it moves downhill. When the slab shatters, slows, and stops, it can bury everything in its way deep in cement-like snow.

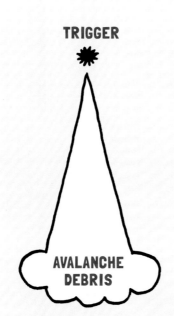

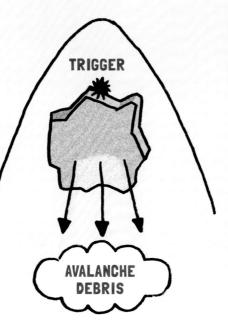

THE FOUR MAIN INGREDIENTS OF A SLAB AVALANCHE

1. Slab: A thick layer of snow that might begin to move in one piece.

2. Bed surface: A smooth, slippery layer that the slab could slide over.

3. Angle: Avalanches are most likely to occur on slopes of thirty to fifty degrees. The most common angle is thirty-eight degrees, slightly steeper than a playground slide.

4. Trigger: Something that will push on the snow to make it start moving. This can be the weight of a person, an animal, or new snow; a wind gust; or an explosion.

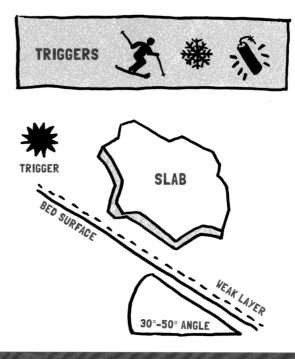

Sniff the Snow

Crystal Mountain and other ski resorts need the best avalanche searchers—and that means dogs! With fast legs and a sharp nose, a dog like Piper can search an area in a half hour that would take twenty people four hours to search.

THE SCIENCE OF SMELL: HOW DOGS' NOSES WORK

Dogs make terrific searchers because they can smell forty-four times better than humans. Here's why:

- The outside of a dog's nose is spongy and wet, which absorbs the scent out of the air.

- Dogs smell out of each nostril separately, which helps them tell where the scent is coming from.

- Inside a dog's nose, a fold of tissue acts like a little gate that separates air into two areas. Some air goes into the lungs for breathing and some goes into a special smelling compartment. The smelling compartment has more than 200 million smell receptors. That's forty times more receptors than humans have!

- When people breathe, air goes in and out of the same part of the nose (the nostrils). While dogs inhale through their nostrils, they exhale through little slits to the side of the nostrils. The air exhaled through the side slits actually pushes new odors into the nostrils.

- A huge fraction—a full one-eighth—of a dog's brain processes smell, making them true smelling geniuses!

Meet the Class

Piper's day starts with a morning meeting in the ski patrol office. Piper runs in, tail wagging, and greets the other dogs and ski patrollers.

Piper's class, called a team, is small—just five dogs total. Three of the dogs are already certified for avalanche rescue. They are:

CERTIFIED

ARI

KALA

CERTIFIED

RIKI

CERTIFIED

A sweet ten-year-old Guide Dogs for the Blind candidate turned rescue dog, Ari is a nonstop tail wagger who loves people. This black Labrador retriever will probably retire and relax at home with his owner after this season.

Kala is a shy, sensitive, big chocolate Lab. She can seem mopey until it's time to hit the snow! Then she comes to life, ready to search and rescue.

This bossy, all-business nine-year-old chocolate Lab is the best search dog on the team, and she knows it. When Riki hops on a dog bed, all the other dogs clear out.

Best Friends Forever

Piper is training for certification alongside Darwin, her best friend. Darwin is the class clown. He barks a lot. (He has a lot to say!) He whines when he's leashed. (Who likes leashes?) And he plays with things he's not supposed to. (Socks are yummy . . .) The five-year-old Nova Scotia duck tolling retriever was born on Valentine's Day, and Piper adores him.

RESCUE PUPPIES

Not every puppy has what it takes to become an avalanche rescue dog. Avalanche rescue dogs must be smart, agile, athletic, and eager to please. They need thick pads on their paws and dense hair to protect them from the cold. It also helps if they are small and light enough to be carried.

Usually handlers choose their dogs from a breeder. But Piper didn't come from a breeder. She was a shelter rescue who seemed to be afraid of everything. On Sara's first hike with the pup, Piper barked at big trees, other dogs, and people. With calming cues and lots of treats, Sara tried to teach her to be less afraid. Piper began to calm down. "I felt like Piper was saying to me: 'I'm afraid, but I trust you, and I can learn how to do this,'" Sara says. That is exactly the attitude a rescue dog in training needs.

Piper's best friend Darwin, pictured here, was adopted for the program from a breeder when he was just eight weeks old.

Up the Mountain

To get to class at the top of the mountain, Piper and her classmates ride a gondola or chairlift. Piper was terrified her first time riding a gondola. Sara had to pick her up and carry her into it. Once on the gondola, the pup plastered herself to the floor and refused to look out the window. But after lots of training and lots of treats, the gondola became a regular part of Piper's morning commute. These days, she gazes excitedly out the window searching for fox tracks in the fresh snow.

Piper also rides chairlifts. Just like skiers and snowboarders, Piper waits in line. When it's their turn, Sara signals Piper forward. As the chairlift comes up behind them, Sara says, "Load up," and Piper hops on as if she is hopping on a couch. Sara pets her as they soar high above the snow. Piper's ears flap and her tail fluffs in the wind.

Sara doesn't just care for Piper. She is Piper's teacher, called a *handler*. (Each dog on the team has a handler.) Sara teaches Piper all the skills she needs to be a rescue dog, and she will work with Piper on real rescues when she's ready.

15

The Basics

Before people learn to read, they need to recognize letters. And before they can add, they need to be able to count. Piper, Darwin, and their classmates need to learn some basics too.

Sit!

Get into a seated position.

Down!

Lie down.

THE POWER OF TREATS AND TUGS

All the handlers keep dog treats and rope tugs in their lockers and backpacks. That's because they reinforce behaviors they want with rewards. To teach Piper a new cue, Sara says a cue such as "Sit!" and rewards Piper with a treat or a game of tug whenever the pup follows it correctly.

Stay!

Hold the position until released.

Catch it!

Grab a toy
from the air.

But that's just the beginning. Piper has learned an astounding eighty cues. Piper can:

Paw!

Raise a paw.

Spin!

Make a complete circle.

Touch!

Press nose to Sara's hand.

Go through!

Go through legs as directed.

She can "Stop" on a dime and "Reverse" (walk back-ward). And she's working on "Slow" (walking VERY slowly), "Bow" (front elbows down, butt up), and even "Dance" (walking on two back legs).

Down the Mountain

Piper and her friends even take skiing lessons. They don't use skis, boots, and poles, but they do have to learn how to run down the mountain as their handlers ski. To teach Piper to get into a position where she would be sheltered between Sara's legs, Sara stands on a flat area with her skis in a wedge shape like a slice of pizza. She says, "In," and rewards Piper when she hops over a ski and in between Sara's legs. Then Sara says, "Out," and rewards Piper for hopping outside the skis. Then Sara practices the cue while moving slowly downhill, then faster, then faster.

To get down a steep slope safely, Sara must turn back and forth. Piper learns that if Sara points her pole out in front and yells, "Turn," she needs to switch sides. These days, Piper can dance all around Sara as she speeds down the slope.

All that learning can get tiring. So Piper and her friends get recess several times a day. Piper and Darwin's favorite thing to do is **PLAY!**

Quiet Time

When Piper, Darwin, and other team members get pooped, they head into a hut to warm up and relax.

Preparing to Search

When Piper is good and rested, it's time for her most important lesson of the day—an avalanche rescue drill.

Piper has been learning how to search for people buried under snow since she was eight months old. Sara started out with easy hide-and-seek games. Someone would hide nearby. Sara said, "Search," and Piper ran to the "victim." Then the victim hid farther and farther away, and then behind trees, and then behind snowbanks. Eventually, Piper could sniff out where a patroller hid in a snow cave.

To prepare for the certification test, Piper and Sara run drills that mimic real-life rescues. The training team sets up the drill on a field of debris left by an avalanche that was triggered by patrollers. The area is almost one hundred meters by one hundred meters, as wide as two football fields, with big, jagged snow boulders jutting up at all angles.

Darwin's handler, Kim, digs a snow cave, like a tiny room under the snow. Then another patroller Andi climbs inside, and Kim completely covers the hole with snow. They are very careful not to touch the surface snow with their bodies, and they ski all over the site to cover their tracks.

Piper will have to maneuver around lots of large chunks of avalanche debris. And wind blowing through the bumpy surface will scatter Andi's scent, making it harder for Piper to find the victim.

BOOM! HOW SKI PATROLLERS KEEP PEOPLE SAFE FROM AVALANCHES

Avalanche specialists at ski resorts monitor snow conditions constantly. They consider all the factors that could make the snowpack unstable, such as:

- New snow adding weight that could slide

- Winds blowing snow into deep, heavy drifts

- Rain that adds water, increasing the snowpack's weight

- Temperature changes, especially freezing and thawing cycles, that create slick surfaces or weak layers over which new snow layers could slide

When specialists identify avalanche danger areas, patrollers sometimes purposely trigger an avalanche before opening those trails. To clear the area where Sara and Piper will run this drill, patrollers throw twenty-five pounds of explosives on the snow. A fuse burns for ninety seconds, and then there's a huge BOOM!

The snow heaves up from the shock waves. The smooth surface shatters, like a cracking pane of glass. A big slab of snow begins slipping slowly downhill. It speeds up as powder billows up around it. The snow slides more than 400 feet (122 meters) before coming to rest. And no one is trapped or hurt.

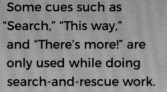

Some cues such as "Search," "This way," and "There's more!" are only used while doing search-and-rescue work.

Search!

On the upper right corner of the big snow field, they are ready to start. Sara kneels down and gently holds Piper's vest. Sara positions her body so they both face downhill. Excitement builds. Then Sara says softly, almost in a whisper: "Search."

Piper bolts away, sprinting down the hill. She lowers her head to sniff the snow, raises it to survey the area, and lowers it again. She runs all the way across the wide debris field to the other side—and out of the avalanche area! Sara wonders why.

Did something distract her?

HOW IS A SCENT LIKE COLOR?

All humans are smelly, at least to dogs. Human scent is a mixture of sweat, dead skin, bacteria, and soaps. Handlers talk about how strong or "bright" the scent is. They train rescue dogs to be able to track both bright and "dim" (or weak) scents.

- A person emits a bright scent.

- A piece of clothing that person wore has a dimmer scent.

- The scent when a person is buried near the surface will be bright.

- The scent of someone buried deeper in the snow will be dimmer on the surface.

Dogs know they are on the right track when they run in a direction and the scent gets brighter—and when they dig down and the scent gets brighter still.

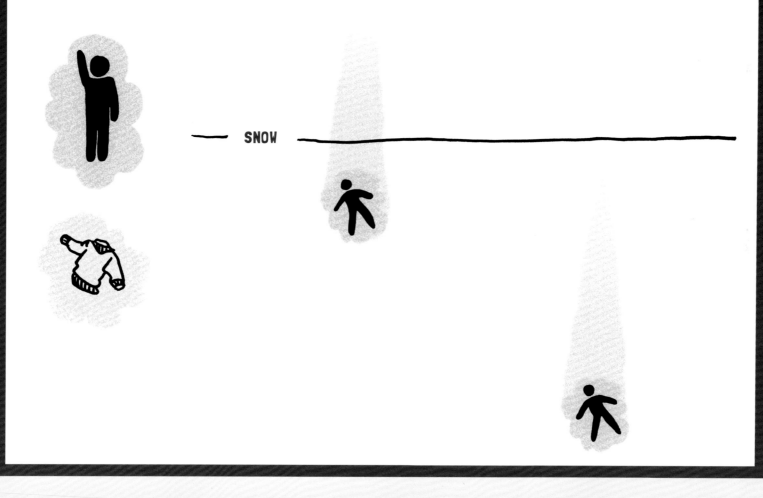

SNOW

Off Track

Piper searches around some trees and then returns to the avalanche area, working her way through the chunks, circling some large snow boulders, sniffing as she goes.

Piper crisscrosses the field twice. But when she reaches the edge, she keeps going, off the avalanche field into the smooth powder again.

"Piper, this way!" Sara calls. Sara turns her body to face the avalanche area, trying to signal to Piper to return to the debris field. Piper looks up but continues climbing the smooth snow beside the avalanche debris. Sara lets her. Sometimes rescue dogs have to sniff off the avalanche site to detect the edge of a scent that is being blown away from the buried person.

Piper zigzags slowly uphill, climbing high above the debris field. She turns slightly toward the avalanche area and stops. She sniffs. For a moment Piper doesn't move.

WIND AND THE SCENT CONE

A person's scent is strongest and most concentrated nearby the source. As the scent is blown by the wind, it spreads in an ever-narrower shape called a scent cone.

On a still day, a dog must pass close to a buried person to pick up a scent cone, but it will be a bright scent.

On a day with light wind, the scent cone will extend across a longer area.

On a very windy day, the scent cone will stretch far across the avalanche field but in a dim and narrow band that is challenging to detect.

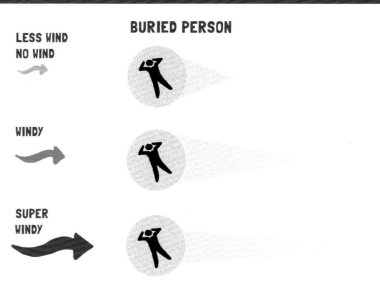

BURIED PERSON

LESS WIND
NO WIND

WINDY

SUPER
WINDY

30

Head down, she sniffs again. Then she sprints down the hill onto the avalanche field and beelines straight for the buried patroller. She is there in seconds. Right on top of the snow cave, Piper halts, then barks and digs at the snow to signal her discovery.

Inside the hole, Andi hears sniffing, barking, and digging. Some soft snow sprinkles down, and the opening gets lighter and lighter. Then Piper's snout pushes through. She did it!

"Good girl, Piper!" Andi calls.

Now the fun begins. Andi rewards Piper by jiggling a bright braided tug toy. Piper grabs it in her mouth and pulls and tugs. Andi tugs back playfully until Piper pulls them both out of the hole. And then they play some more.

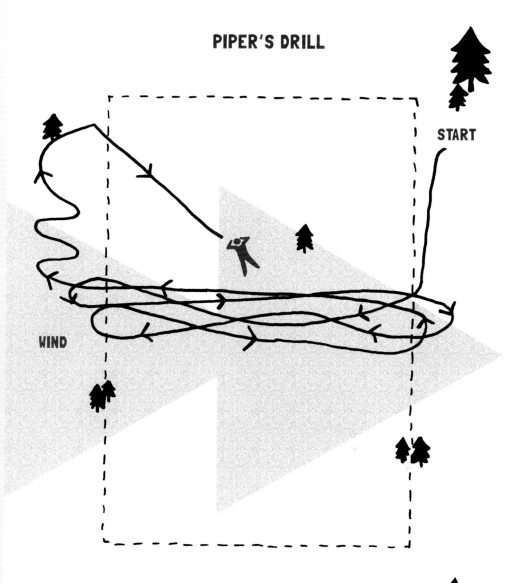

PIPER'S DRILL

START

WIND

Rescue-dog handlers and ski patrollers Sara Cohen and Kim Haft (right) discuss Piper and Darwin's progress.

Is Piper Ready?

The official avalanche rescue certification test will be even more challenging. Piper will have to find two people buried in two different snow caves. Three sweaters that have absorbed human scent will be buried in shallow holes, and she must locate two of them. And she'll have to do all of this in just forty minutes.

All winter long, Sara and Piper practice. Toward the end of the season, Sara thinks Piper is ready. But she's not sure. "Conditions can be really tough this late in the season," Sara says. Spring means mushy snow, and running through mush can be tiring. And if Piper gets hot, panting will interfere with her ability to smell.

It's also possible that Piper is still too young. Younger dogs are more easily distracted—and Piper is so social, she wants to greet everyone she sees. She's also sensitive to loud noises.

But Sara decides to give her a chance.

The Big Test

On test day, Sara and Piper wake early. Sara spends a little extra time brushing Piper to calm them both.

At the ski resort, Kim and a team of patrollers bury two people in snow caves and three scented sweaters in a large snowy area away from all the ski trails. (To pass the test, Piper will need to find both people and two out of three of the sweaters.)

Sara and Piper don't know where the test site is located. In fact, Piper has never been there before, which adds to the challenge.

As the pair waits together in the patrol hut for the test to begin, Sara is excited but a little nervous too, her stomach churning. "I have to keep cool for Piper. She can smell stress, so if I'm stressed, she'll get stressed."

The Call for Help

Suddenly Sara's radio blares: "This is an avalanche drill. Code two. Meet the witness at the run out of Elizabeth Lake."

Sara calls Piper out of her kennel, hurries into her skis, and scoops Piper into her arms. She wants to save Piper's energy for the search.

Kim waits for them at the bottom of a slope near Elizabeth Lake. The sun shines bright and hot, but a cold wind sweeps across the frozen lake and up the vast hill. Kim points frantically at the slope, pretending to have witnessed an avalanche that caught some skiers. "I saw four, maybe five people." Kim says.

A few other ski patrollers arrive carrying long poles called probes that they can push into the snow to locate someone buried deep below.

"Stay here," Sara tells Kim. "We're going to begin searching."

She lets Piper off the leash and crouches down next to her, facing the huge search area. "Piper, this is it!" Sara says. Piper snaps to attention. "We have a lot of WORK to do."

Piper steps a paw forward.

"SEARCH!"

Kim starts the clock.

Did She Smell Something?

Piper bounds through the snow, weaving up the slope. She heads into the middle, running fast.

Suddenly, she stops and her head snaps back. Did she smell something? She sniffs a bit but continues across the slope toward a cluster of trees.

Sara trudges higher up the hill. The wind is blowing up slope, so Sara wants to position Piper where the scent will drift toward her. "Piper, this way!" she calls.

But Piper ignores her and runs back to the middle of the slope, where she had paused before. She stops and sniffs. But she doesn't dig or bark.

Is someone buried there? Sara is allowed to enlist two patrollers to probe the snow. "Can I get a prober down here?" she yells. While the patroller pokes the snow, she and Piper continue to search the far side of the slope.

Behind them, the prober calls: "Got a **STRIKE!**"

"Three minutes, twenty-two seconds," Kim yells. Piper was right. She located a person buried in a snow cave in just over three minutes!

Dig, Dig, Dig

Piper spends a few minutes in the smooth powder outside the search area. Sara lets her sniff there for a while.

Suddenly, Piper turns and runs straight to a spot, sticks her nose in the snow, sniffs and digs furiously, snow flying.

Sara rushes over. Piper yanks a sweater out of the snow.

"Oh, oh, oh!" Sara calls in a singsong tone. "Nice job, Piper!"

She yells to Kim: "We have a **STRIKE!**" Elapsed time is under eight minutes.

Sara kneels down next to Piper and plays tug with her, crooning, "Good job! Good job, Piper! Oh, what a good job!"

Back to Work

But the clock is still ticking. The pup still has another person and another article of clothing to find. Sara tucks the sweater into her backpack and says, "Back to work."

Piper dips her head to the ground, sniffs, and trots off down the slope. She weaves around then picks up speed. She heads straight for something. She circles a spot, stops, and digs.

Sara skis away, but Piper won't follow her. She keeps digging. Sara reads this as victim loyalty, a clear signal that Piper thinks she has found someone and she is not going to leave until help comes.

"Can I get a prober down here?" Sara calls.

The patroller comes and starts poking the snow, and Sara redirects Piper. "There's more," she says intently.

Piper heads back toward the center of the slope. She lifts her head up to sniff the air.

Behind her, the prober yells, "**STRIKE!**" Piper was right about where the second person was buried! Elapsed time: Nine minutes, two seconds. Piper only has to find one more of the two remaining sweaters to pass the test!

Distracted

She scampers and sniffs, turns and sniffs. But then **SCREEECH!** off in the distance, a snowmobile alarm goes off. Piper stops. The alarm ends, but Piper still doesn't move. She seems frozen.

Sara hopes Piper will return to searching, but she doesn't. Time ticks down.

Sara calls out, a plea in a high-pitched voice: "Get to work, Piper!"

Piper gazes toward her. She pauses, then Piper slowly weaves up the hill toward Sara. She sniffs left. She sniffs right. She trots left. She trots right. Then she stops.

Piper wheels around and bolts down the slope.

Near the bottom, Piper pounces into the snow and starts digging joyfully with both paws, snow flying between her back legs. She proudly pulls a sweater out of the snow.

Sara yells, "**STRIKE!**"

Kim calls out, "Sixteen minutes and thirty-one seconds!"

Sara skis down fast, hooting and hollering: "Wha-ha-ha! Weeeeee! OH, GOOD PIPER!"

Piper answers with a joyful, "BARK, BARK, BARK!"

A call rings out over the ski patrol radio: "Congratulations to Piper! She has passed her certification test!"

Everyone cheers.

Kim and Sara high-five.

Piper barks and pokes Sara with her nose.

"Good girl," Sara says. And she gives Piper a kiss on the head.

Dog Tired

At the end of the day, after the lifts close, all the patrollers ski down the mountain to make sure no one's stranded on the slopes. Piper sprints down the hill next to Sara for this final sweep.

Everyone gathers again in the ski patrol office. Piper says hi to all her human friends, hoping for belly rubs. She greets her best friend Darwin who is scouring the place for leftovers to swipe. Piper buries her head in Sara's smelly ski boot. Darwin barks at lockers to point out that they hold yummy treats inside. And the two furry friends have one last tug.

As the sun sets, everyone takes off their uniforms, closes up their lockers, and says goodbye. After a long day and a job well done, Piper and Sara head home for dinner, an extra snuggle, and bedtime.

Piper needs to rest up for the days ahead because now she is ready to be a real avalanche rescue dog hero.

MAKE YOUR OWN TUG TOY

The rescue dogs love these homemade toys. They are bright so they stand out in the snow. The fluffy fringes are exciting when they are shaken. The fleece feels good on their gums. And the knots give them something to hold so they can TUG!

Rather than buy expensive toys, the handlers make their own. Here's how:

- Buy one-fourth yard each of three different colors of fleece from a fabric store.

- Cut the fleece into four- to six-inch-wide strips, each two and a half feet long.

- Cut some three-inch-long fringes on each end.

- Knot together three different strips of fleece at one end, just below the fringes.

- Braid the fleece.

- Knot the other end, leaving dangling fringes.

- For added excitement, cut the fringes into thinner strips.

- If the tug is too long, tie a knot or two in the center.

TRAIN YOUR DOG TO TUG

If you play tug with your dog, you should follow a few rules to make the game safe and fun for you both.

- You should always initiate the game, but let your dog decide whether or not to play.

- Offer the tug in a way that gives the dog enough room to grab it without putting teeth too near your hand.

- Invite the dog to grab it by using a cue such as "Let's play!"

- Play gently. Tug only side-to-side and not up-and-down, and with only as much force as the dog puts in.

- Never try to make your dog mad by poking, hitting, or growling.

- If the dog's teeth touch your skin or clothes, even if by accident, calmly stop the game immediately.

- To teach your dog to let go of the tug, pick one cue such as "Let go," "Leave it," "Drop," or "Give." Stop tugging, freeze, and say the cue, while holding a food treat near the dog's nose. When the dog releases the toy, offer praise and the treat. Soon the pup will release the toy without a treat.

Piper also recently passed her Backcountry Avalanche Rescue K9s (BARK) certification! Now she can use her search skills all across Washington State.

Resources

READ MORE

Goodman, Susan E. *It's a Dog's Life: How Man's Best Friend Sees, Hears, and Smells the World.* New York: Flash Point, 2012.

Horowitz, Alexandra. *Inside of a Dog: What Dogs See, Smell, and Know.* Young Readers ed. New York: Simon & Schuster, 2016.

O'Bannon, Allen and Mike Clelland. *Allen & Mike's Avalanche Book: A Guide to Staying Safe in Avalanche Terrain.* Guilford: FalconGuides, 2012.

Patent, Dorothy Hinshaw. *Super Sniffers: Dog Detectives on the Job.* New York: Bloomsbury, 2014.

SURF MORE

Follow Piper and the rest of the Crystal Mountain rescue team on social media:
Facebook—@CrystalMountainAvalancheRescueDogs
Instagram—@cm_avydogs

Watch a short video of Darwin at work: bit.ly/2ijo80A

Find your avalanche forecast nationwide: www.avalanche.org

Check the avalanche forecast for the Pacific Northwest at the Northwest Avalanche Center: www.nwac.us

Watch an animated TED Talk on how dogs' noses work: bit.ly/1LEppad

Learn more about how scent moves with airflow: bit.ly/1yHmvcM

Catch an award-winning video on the rescue dogs of Telluride Ski Resort in Colorado: bit.ly/2julKaS

Check out these adorable videos of avalanche rescue PUPPIES in training:
bit.ly/2muRbTp | bit.ly/2mtUjPj | bit.ly/1wvRDJ9

Acknowledgments

THANKS TEAM!

It takes a team to make a book. My first thanks go to editor Christy Cox for committing so quickly to this idea and to Christy, Bridget Sweet, and Bryce de Flamand for their support, wisdom, and general brilliance throughout the process. Thanks to my two writing critique groups (the Downtown Group and the Viva Scrivas) for their sage advice, and to writer's assistant extraordinaire Liz Goss for the amazing graphics she prepared for the book and other contributions.

My deep appreciation to the members of the Crystal Mountain Ski Patrol and avalanche dog rescue teams for opening their huts and their hearts to help me tell this story, especially Rikki Dunn, Michael Haft, Kim Kircher, Miles Morris, Andi Nelson, David Seal, Rich Starrett, and Bud Stevens.

Every time I look at the photos of Piper and her friends, I smile. My sincere thanks to photographer Dylan Cembalski for his beautiful work and to photographer Lynne Spencer for her stamina and good cheer during an epic few days that included skiing downhill fast while shooting Piper in motion with a new camera. I'm so glad you didn't crash.

For making the most of these photos and unlocking their storytelling possibilities, thank you to photo editor and creative consultant Karin Anderson. It is always a joy to collaborate with you.

Final thanks to Sara Cohen and her Oreo Piper, and to Kim Haft and her gingersnap Darwin. These humans and canines were extremely patient, extremely helpful, and extremely inspiring. The skiers and snowboarders of Crystal Mountain Resort are lucky to have you watching out for them. And so was I.

SUPPORT THE HEROES

Funding for the training and care of the avalanche rescue dogs is provided by the 501(c)(3) nonprofit Cascade Mountain Rescue Dogs. Donations help pay for the dogs' health insurance, special off-mountain trainings, and search-and-rescue missions outside Crystal Mountain.

The sale of annual rescue-dog shirts and hoodies also supports the team's efforts. Shirts and hoodies are available for purchase in the aid room at ski patrol for Crystal Mountain Resort or at the Country Animal Hospital in Enumclaw, Washington. They can also be ordered and shipped to you. Inquire about donations or shirt orders at: cm.rescuedogs@gmail.com.

Mail checks to: Cascade Mountain Rescue Dogs, P.O. Box 664, Enumclaw, WA 98022.
The dogs and handlers thank you for your support!

Manufactured in China by C&C Offset Printing Co. Ltd.
Shenzhen, Guangdong Province, in June 2018

22 21 20 19 18   9 8 7 6 5 4 3 2 1

Editor: Christy Cox
Production editor: Bridget Sweet
Design: Bryce de Flamand

Cover photographs: Dylan Cembalski (front), Lynne Spencer (back)
End sheet photographs: Dylan Cembalski (front, middle), Lynne Spencer (back)
Interior photographs: Dylan Cembalski (pages 2–9, 11, 15 [top], 17 [top], 20, 23, 24 [left], 25–26, 28–29, 34–37, 40–44), Kim Kircher (page 25 [box]), Chris Morin (page 13), Cobi Rusch (page 48), Lynne Spencer (pages 1,10, 12, 14, 15 [bottom], 16, 17 [bottom], 18, 21–22, 24 [right], 30, 32–33, 38–39, 46)
Photo editor: Karin Anderson
Graphics: Elizabeth Goss and Bryce de Flamand

Library of Congress Cataloging-in-Publication Data

Names: Rusch, Elizabeth, author.
Title: Avalanche dog heroes / Elizabeth Rusch.
Description: Seattle : Little Bigfoot, [2018]
Identifiers: LCCN 2018000291 | ISBN 9781632171733 (hardcover)
Subjects: LCSH: Rescue dogs—Training—Washington (State)—Crystal Mountain—Juvenile literature. | Avalanches—Juvenile literature.
Classification: LCC SF428.55 .R87 2018 | DDC 636.7/088609797—dc23
LC record available at https://lccn.loc.gov/2018000291

ISBN: 978-1-63217-173-3

Sasquatch Books | 1904 Third Avenue, Suite 710 | Seattle, WA 98101
(206) 467-4300 | SasquatchBooks.com

For Reba, my canine hero

Get More Out of This Book

GROUP DISCUSSION

- Discuss with children what they might already know about avalanches.

- Locate Crystal Mountain Resort on a digital map. Talk about this being the setting of the book.

- After reading the book, discuss the ways dogs and people rely on each other. Ask, "What are some other ways dogs help people?" Teach the protocol of never approaching a service dog without the owner's permission because the dog is "working" for the human and needs to stay focused.

- Discuss why dog handlers use one-word or two-word commands. What might the reasoning be behind that choice? Why might a K9 handler use a foreign language, such as German, with their dog?

- After reading the book, discuss something new that children learned about either avalanches or rescue dogs.

- Encourage children to make a personal connection to the story by discussing how their school day might be the same or different from Piper and Darwin's.

- Discuss why time was an important criterion during Piper's training.

In reference to the diagram showing the two main types of avalanches, think about how you could explain how avalanches occur by using the Next Generation Science Standards crosscutting concept of cause and effect. Consider the sentence stems of:

1.   _(cause)_ causes   _(effect)_ .

2.   An effect of   _(cause)_   is   _____ .

3.   Avalanches (effect) can happen when   _(cause)_ .

INDEPENDENT ACTIVITIES

- Ask children to think of ways technology could help save lives and/or locate people caught in an avalanche. Have children research avalanche beacons and airbags using the internet and then design a device of their own for either dogs or humans. Think about the limitations of testing such devices as well as the cost of materials.

- Write a résumé for the ideal rescue dog. Discuss the implications of training dogs from the Humane Society to become rescue dogs. What qualities do Sara and her colleagues look for in dogs?

- If you have a pet dog at home, think about how you could train it to do a task or "trick" for you. What steps would you take to make it happen? Think about how Sara trained Piper. What did she use as rewards for Piper? Consider writing a protocol using the adverbs *first*, *next*, *then*, and *last*. Stay dedicated to your protocol for a month and see what happens!

EDUCATOR'S GUIDE

These discussion questions and activities can be found in a downloadable educator's guide on our website. Please visit the Little Bigfoot Resources page on our website to find this and other educator resources for our children's books: SasquatchBooks.com

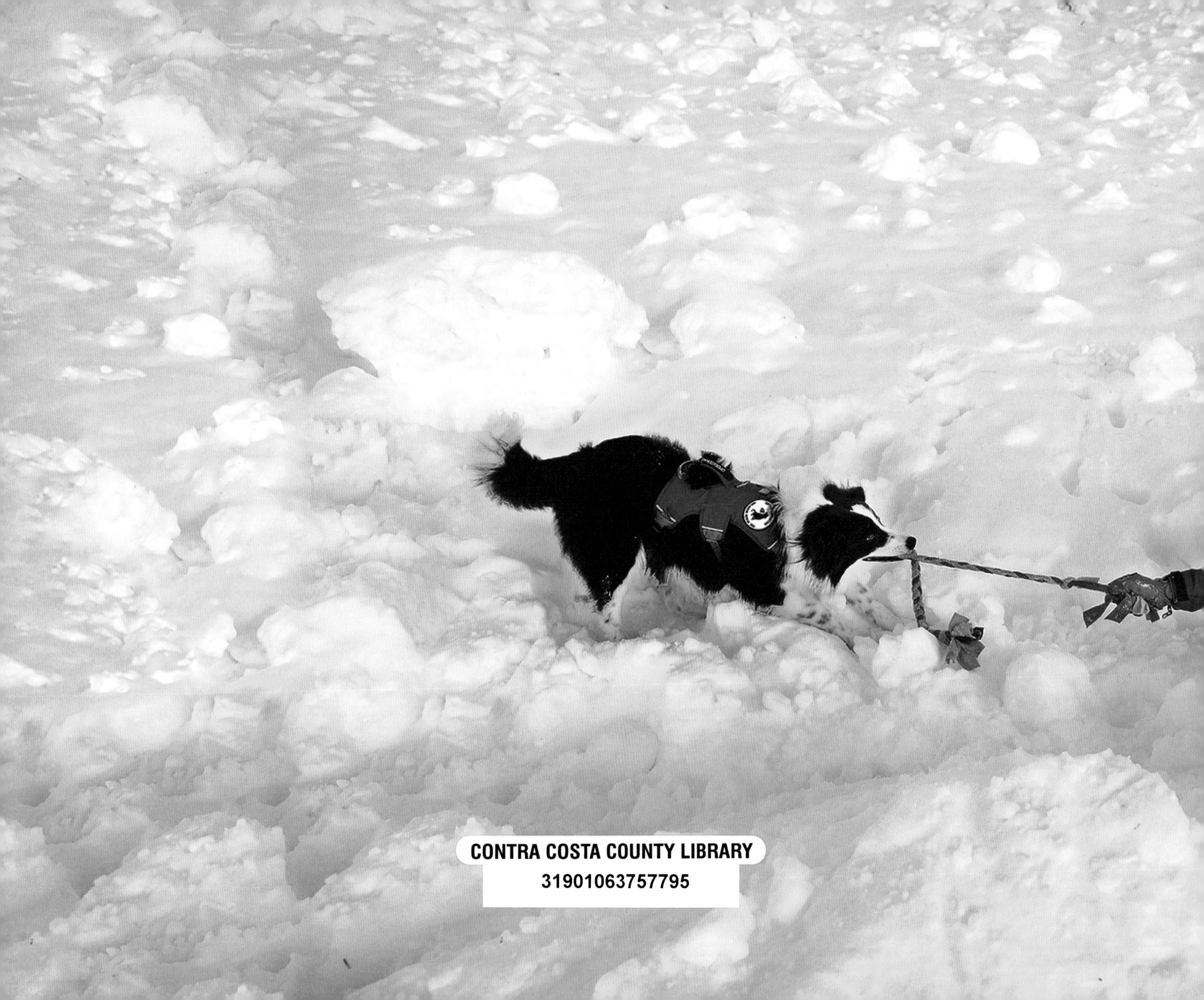